A MONTH OF SUNDAYS

Dr. Malcolm Burton

1   2   3

10

7   8   9

14   15   16   17

CONTENTS

Foreword

Changes.

Life contains changes.

My life has been no exception.

Much of this writing was done as a Pastor.

Today I find myself involved in foreign missions.

The commonality of this and my ministry in the U.S. is The Word.

The Word of God is central to everything I have done and everything I will ever do on planet earth.

Please allow the simple truth of these exhortations to encourage your emotional life, stir your faith, and renew your energy.

Much better days lie ahead.

Believe and say aloud that truth.

Thank you for reading my book.

I pray you'll be blessed.

Dr. Malcolm Burton
School of The Holy Spirit
Madison County, Texas
June, 2018

1
"I Just Vant To Talk Vit You!"
(Today's Devotion is Taken From Luke 2:8-20)

I have been to the cave.

Yes, The Cave of The Shepherds.

This is a favorite Christmas memory.

Pardon me for telling it again...but it is fun!

Besides, you know how it is with we preachers.

Illustrations have no shelf-life and don't wear out.

Back To The Bible Account

Ancient Shepherds would feed their sheep by day.

At night they would drive the sheep into a huge cave.

The day I was in the cave I was joined by about 200 people.

A safe place from rain, cold weather, predators and thieves, the cave has a natural fireplace.

Some scholars believe the cave is in close proximity to The Tower of Eder where spotless lambs were kept before being offered as a Temple sacrifice.

"Now there were in the same country shepherds living out in the fields, keeping watch over their flock by night. 9 And behold, an angel of the Lord stood before them, and the glory of the Lord shone around them, and they were greatly afraid. 10 Then the angel said to them, "Do not be afraid, for behold, I bring you good tidings of great joy which will be to all people," (Luke 2:8-10).

I was warming myself by the "fireplace" on a particularly cold and damp November evening.

Unexpectedly, a voice spoke out of the chimney. No, it was not the Lord.

It was not The Angel Gabriel, nor was it another member of the heavenly realm.

It was a German tourist attempting to tease the largely American group in the cave.

"I am the Lordt Thy Godt," came the message in Germanic sounding English. "Listen to me. Do not be afraidt. I just vant to talk vit you."

All jokes aside, our Lord still "vants" to talk. He is a communicator Who is greatly interested in the most minute details of our daily life.

"For there is born to you this day in the city of David a Savior, who is Christ the Lord. 12 And this will be the sign to you: You will find a Babe wrapped in swaddling clothes, lying in a manger," (Luke 2:11-12)

Obviously, it was a funny and unforgettable moment I treasure to this day.

The person speaking on that cold winter evening so very long ago was not "the Lordt my Godt" but an angel.

Some scholars theorize about which angel was actually speaking in these verses.

If a guess must be put forth, I would vote for Gabriel, functioning in his role as the Messenger Angel.

A Sign Given

The "sign" was the divestiture of The Christ.

Jesus, King of All, set aside His Divinity, and came to earth.

While not born into poverty, His humility was further expressed in the location and circumstance of His birth.

> *"And suddenly there was with the angel a multitude of the heavenly host praising God and saying: 14 " Glory to God in the highest, And on earth peace, goodwill toward men!"*
> *(Luke 2:13-14).*

Supernatural events occurred simultaneous to the arrival of Jesus on earth. An angelic choir appeared to serenade the Shepherds in the field. The shekinah---*God's visible glory*---hovered above.

Our Lord understands show business!

> *"So it was, when the angels had gone away from them into heaven, that the shepherds said to one another, "Let us now go to Bethlehem and see this thing that has come to pass, which the Lord has made known to us,"* (Luke 2:15).

The Shepherds immediately began seeking to find Jesus. This is a great example to us who have experienced salvation. There is always much more of His grace and knowledge to experience.

No matter how long we walk with Him there remains great personal relationship to be more fully developed.

> *"And they came with haste and found Mary and Joseph, and the Babe lying in a manger," (Luke 2:16).*

Jesus was not born in an awful place. He was born in a place typical of the time. Hotels as we know them today did not exist in those days. Most travelers prevailed on a wealthy family member for lodging.

Thus, Jesus likely was born in a combination of hospitality room and barn.

The animals would be tethered on the dirt floor of the barn with humans lodged on an elevated deck.

> *"Now when they had seen Him, they made widely known the saying which was told them concerning this Child,"*
> *(Luke 2:17).*

The shepherds set into motion one of the essentials of Christianity ...witnessing.

A "Texas Style" Witness

They did not fear the opinions of men.

They had witnessed something precious and felt it was worthy of their sharing.

My East Texas roots and a fertile imagination think what it would be like if the Shepherd's had been Texans.

Imagine asking one of the now elderly shepherds if he had heard of "…that exceptional new preacher, Jesus."

Let your imagination add the soulful strains of drawling deep East Texas speech.

«Heard of Him? I was there the night the boy was born!»

> *"And all those who heard it marveled at those things which were told them by the shepherds. 19 But Mary kept all these things and pondered them in her heart. 20 Then the shepherds returned, glorifying and praising God for all the things that they had heard and seen, as it was told them,"*
> *(Luke 2:18-20).*

Praising and pondering have been part of Christianity for thousands of years. We gather together in this book to ponder the related Scriptures again. We praise Him for what He has done, is doing and will do. We ponder what we do not understand and seek Him. As we seek Him, more understanding comes to us.

In Him is the knowledge of all things.

2

Clothed In His Glory
(Today's Devotion is Taken From Genesis 3:6-11)

The Anointing.

A beautiful term. I asked an old preacher about the anointing of God.

New to the ministry, I wondered about this mystical thing he spoke of. The gentleman pondered my question silently for what seemed to me to be an eternity before replying.

"Honestly, I am not sure I know what the anointing is. But, I certainly do know when I don't have it."

> *"So when the woman saw that the tree was good for food, that it was pleasant to the eyes, and a tree desirable to make one wise, she took of its fruit and ate. She also gave to her husband with her, and he ate," (Genesis 3:6).*

God told Adam and Eve they could have anything they wanted in the Garden.

There was one exception: They were not to eat the fruit of the tree of the knowledge of good and evil. Apparently, God considered being in the presence of wisdom to be enough.

Once again it makes me wonder how many things I have "caught" rather than been "taught."

> *"Then the eyes of both of them were opened, and they knew that they were naked; and they sewed fig leaves together and made themselves coverings," (Genesis 3:7).*

The Perfect Couple rebelled.

They did the only thing they were told not to do. In a moment Adam and Eve lost their innocence. In the perfect Garden of Eden, they had managed to sin.

In their sinless state they had stood before God clothed in His glory...unashamed.

Interestingly, please note how Adam and Eve immediately crafted clothing after sin had damaged their relationship with God.

Like many Christians today, they instantly sought to hide from the only One Who could help.

> *"And they heard the sound of the LORD God walking in the garden in the cool of the day, and Adam and his wife hid themselves from the presence of the LORD God among the trees of the garden," (Genesis 3:8).*

God has always desired fellowship with mankind. Walking in fellowship with God is to be part of each day's activity.

Since the Day of Pentecost and the birthday of the church, such fellowship should be normal for Christians every day.

God desires that we visit with Him...even when we have "blown it" by sinning.

> *"Then the LORD God called to Adam and said to him, "Where are you?" (Genesis 3:9).*

No, God had not lost contact with Adam. God was requiring Adam to identify his state. Today the Holy Spirit is asking us, "Where are you?" He is not asking us to define our geographic location. He is checking on our spiritual condition...*something*

He already knows.

The Holy Spirit is asking this question to stir the separated to do the introspection necessary to be restored.

> *"So he said, "I heard Your voice in the garden, and I was afraid because I was naked; and I hid myself,"*
> *(Genesis 3:10).*

Friend, I understand Adam's feeling. I have had days of feeling naked before the Holy Spirit. There have been more days I have stood before Him with no discomfort.

But, we are always naked before our Lord. Yet, we only seem to notice when we have sinned.

Consider These Facts:

• The Holy Spirit lives within us for us.

• The Holy Spirit rests upon us for others.

• He clothes us in His anointing so others can receive from

• His perfection without being distracted by our imperfection.

> *"And He said, "Who told you that you were naked? Have you eaten from the tree of which I commanded you that you should not eat?" (Genesis 3:11).*

This is an amazing question: *"How do you know you are naked?"*

The anointing of God had left their lives. Like the old preacher, I also know what the anointing of God is. Having goofed up in the past, I can also tell you when it is not present.

If things are not right between you and The Lord, don't leave things that way.

Your restoration is as close as the mention of the Name of Jesus wrapped in a prayer of repentance.

Decisions Decide Direction.

Make sure the anointing is fully covering your life.

Yes, it is what is best for you. But, the lives of others are also depending on the miracles released by your anointing.

3

Speaking Victory When It Is Still Unseen
(Today's Devotion is Based Upon Psalm 3:1-6)

A well-intentioned man spoke.

"I don't say I feel 'OK' when I don't."

Well, just for the record, neither do I.

I do not deny sickness has attacked my body.

I declare sickness cannot prevail against my faith.

Never deny reality. Always deny reality the right to govern.

Instead, choose to be governed by your faith in the Word of God.

> *"LORD, how they have increased who trouble me!*
> *Many are they who rise up against me," (Psalm 3:1).*

King David was in a rough spot. His son, Absalom, had almost seduced the entire nation. David had fled the castle and was living in the countryside. Absalom and a superior number of soldiers were seeking David.

No, they did not want to send David off to the retirement home for kings. The plan was to kill King David and install Absalom as leader of the nation.

> *"Many are they who say of me, "There is no help for him in*
> *God." Selah." (Psalm 3:2).*

David was known as a spiritual man.

He was known to hear the voice of God.

His enemies were taking verbal jabs at David.

"Yeah, the King says he knows God. He'd better know Him!"

> *"But You, O LORD, are a shield for me, My glory and the One who lifts up my head," (Psalm 3:3)*

Notice David's style of speaking. He was not describing his life as "over." No, he was thanking God for protecting him...in advance. Your first step toward establishing the life you desire is learning to govern the words you speak.

> *"I cried to the LORD with my voice, And He heard me from His holy hill. Selah," (Psalm 3:4).*

Thinking is not prayer.

Meditation is not prayer.

Prayer is communication with God.

David makes it clear he voiced his request.

He was amazed that God heard him in heaven.

David knew God was not disconnected from His people.

Giving voice to the promises of God activates your faith.

This also stirs God to act in your behalf.

> *"I lay down and slept; I awoke, for the LORD sustained me," (Psalm 3:5).*

What a statement of faith!

David was surrounded by hostile forces. Instead of panicking, David demonstrated his faith. David demonstrated his faith in an amazing way...he went to sleep.

> *"I will not be afraid of ten thousands of people Who have set them- selves against me all around," (Psalm 3:6).*

Learn from David.

Make a bold declaration of faith.

"No matter what I face, I will not be afraid!"

"I will not be afraid...because my Lord is with me!"

4
Optimistic Urgency
(Today's Devotion is Taken From Ezekiel 37:1-4;7)

I am optimistic about life.

But my optimism is tempered by urgency.

Each year holds the potential for greatness...for those who will choose it.

Why the urgency? I sense the prophetic clock of God ticking... time is passing away.

Each year will only be a year of blessing for those who also see it as a year of becoming.

Five Things To Become

1) Become More Concerned With Ministry Than Mess

> *"The hand of the Lord was on me, and he brought me out by the Spirit of the Lord and set me in the middle of a valley; it was full of bones. 2 He led me back and forth among them, and I saw a great many bones on the floor of the valley, bones that were very dry," (Ezekiel 37:1- 2).*

We must get our focus off "mess."

Get our focus back upon our "message."

Ezekiel saw nothing but death and destruction.

Everywhere he looked there was nothing but dry bones.

Make a concerted effort to stop living in judgment of other people.

Allow the Word of God to mean more to you than the dry bones you see.

2) Become Involved In The Person, Not Their Problem

> *"Then he said to me, "Prophesy to these bones and say to them, 'Dry bones, hear the word of the Lord!" (Vs 4).*

Shift your focus from what is wrong.

Ask the Holy Spirit to help you see solutions.

Most "messed up" people know they are "messed up."

We must bring these people to a saving event then immerse them in process.

The process in which to immerse them is seeking the move of The Holy Spirit.

I am not interested in program driven ministry. I am interested in growth brought about by the move of The Holy Spirit.

Speak God's desired outcome over the person to whom you are ministering

3) Become Increasingly Sensitive To the Presence of God

> *"The hand of the Lord was on me," (Ezekiel 37:1a).*

Can you say, "The hand of the Lord is upon me?"

Are you cognizant of His activity in your life?

Note the phrase, *"...He brought me out..."*

He brought me out of confusion and directionless living.

He brought me into the flow of The Holy Spirit.

Some are making major decisions without consulting God at all.

Ezekiel was hearing from God because he was seeking the will of God.

4) Become Increasingly Honest Before God

"He asked me, "Son of man, can these bones live?" I said, "Sovereign Lord, you alone know." 4 Then he said to me, "Prophesy to these bones and say to them, 'Dry bones, hear the word of the Lord!" (Ezekiel 37:3-4).

When God asks you a question He is not seeking your counsel.

He is trying to give you an opportunity to think something through.

God was asking Ezekiel if he believed He could bring His promises to pass.

Your dry bones situation may be relational. Speak to that friendship or marriage and call it back to life.

Your bank account may be a collection of dry bones. Speak to it and tell it to come back to fullness and vitality.

5) Be More Diligent About Speaking Your Desired Result

"So I prophesied as I was commanded. And as I was prophesying, there was a noise, a rattling sound, and the bones came together, bone to bone," (Ezekiel 37:7).

You may be just hearing a 'bunch of noise."

Listen again...and focus. Your hearing will clarify.

You will hear "rattling" before you see things coming together.

But hang on...you will see your desired result.

5
Blundering Into The Glory
(Today's Devotion is Taken From Isaiah 60)

Another Day.

This does not have to be just another year.

But we must choose to use our faith to make it exceptional.

It is my closely held belief that God always desires to "move" on behalf of His people. The past several years of economic misery and uncertainty stirred many to pray and believe for miracles as never before.

As is often the case with me, I feel as if I have "blundered" into something exceptional. What I desire most is in the glory...that season when God visits a person or place for a protracted period of time.

If you want to receive something you have never received you must be willing to go somewhere you have never been.

I have been in the glory before. Going there and staying there is something even more profound...and staying there is my goal.

Six Facts About The Glory

1) The Glory Brings Restoration

> *"Lift up your eyes all around, and see: They all gather together, they come to you; Your sons shall come from afar,*

And your daughters shall be nursed at your side,"
(Isaiah 60:4).

Far too many families are bound by strife.

Harsh words and often recalled things from the past keep the flames of incorrect passion burning.

In the glory, you can find the grace you need to let go, forgive yourself and others and move on.

Things which cannot be humanly restored are routinely made better than new in the glory.

2) The Glory Brings Financial Increase To The House Of God

"All the flocks of Kedar shall be gathered together to you, The rams of Nebaioth shall minister to you; They shall ascend with acceptance on My altar, And I will glorify the house of My glory," (Isaiah 60:7).

Pastoral families have suffered unnecessarily. My former congregation was no exception in the financial area. Inconsistent giving placed our church, and many others, in an unnecessarily financially stressed condition.

When the glory brings financial increase, the House of God begins to prosper. I'm not really speaking of salaries. We, and most other churches, have never had the money needed for effective outreach.

Let me point out something that should excite everyone: The church does not prosper until the people prosper.

Get ready for the glory to cause your Seed to come into fullness.

3) The Glory Will Cause The Churches Throughout The Earth To Experience Revival

> *"Who are these who fly like a cloud, And like doves to their roosts? 9 Surely the coastlands shall wait for Me; And the ships of Tarshish will come first, To bring your sons from afar, Their silver and their gold with them, To the name of the Lord your God, And to the Holy One of Israel, Because He has glorified you," (Isaiah 60:8-9) .*

Many nations of earth have been actively involved in missionary activities at great expense and sacrifice. The harvest is at hand.

The nations that have received missionaries are beginning to send missionaries. The cycle is nearing completion and The Rapture of The Church is more certain than ever.

4) The Glory Will Release Favor From People Unlike You

> *"The sons of foreigners shall build up your walls, And their kings shall minister to you; For in My wrath I struck you, But in My favor I have had mercy on you. 11 Therefore your gates shall be open continually; They shall not be shut day or night, That men may bring to you the wealth of the Gentiles, And their kings in procession. 12 For the nation and kingdom which will not serve you shall perish, And those nations shall be utterly ruined," (Ezekiel 60:10-12).*

Favor is very real and totally unfair to the forces of hell.

It is fashionable to disparage Pat Robertson these days. I choose to remember better days. Pat made a remarkable statement, "If I could only ask God for one thing I would ask Him for favor."

One Day of Favor is Worth 1,000 Days of Labor!

During the manifest glory, business opportunities will flow around the clock. Be kind to the foreigner within your gates. Some are kings. Some are connected to other kings.

The glory upon you will cause them to favor you without knowing why.

5) **In The Glory, Things Are As They Should Be**

> *"Instead of bronze I will bring gold, Instead of iron I will bring silver, Instead of wood, bronze, And instead of stones, iron. I will also make your officers peace, And your magistrates righteousness. 18 Violence shall no longer be heard in your land, Neither wasting nor destruction within your borders; But you shall call your walls Salvation, And your gates Praise," (Isaiah 60:17-18).*

Many have worked hard but produced relatively little.

Many have been faithful to the tithe but have not seen much of a financial harvest. In the glory you see things as they should be and your faith rises to such a place that you can "believe" the blessings into being.

The glory will cause justice to manifest in your life.

The glory will also release supernatural protection against violence and financial downturns.

6) **Jesus Is Free To Manifest In His Fullness When The Glory Is Released.**

> *"The sun shall no longer be your light by day, Nor for brightness shall the moon give light to you; But the Lord will be to you an everlasting light, And your God your glory. 20 Your sun shall no longer go down, Nor*

shall your moon withdraw itself; For the Lord will be your everlasting light, And the days of your mourning shall be ended. 21 Also your people shall all be righteous; They shall inherit the land forever, The branch of My planting, The work of My hands, That I may be glorified," (Isaiah 60:19-21).

God is glorious in and of Himself.

Yes, we should give Him the glory He deserves in our praise and worship. But there is an often-overlooked aspect of His life I would like for us to consider.

God is actually glorified when His people are blessed.

When the glory is released the atmosphere is conditioned for Jesus to really be Jesus.

Where do I wish to go and stay for a sustained period of time? You know it. The Glory!

6
A Prepared Place
(Today's Devotion is Taken From Matthew 28:16-20)

Consider the lyrics to "Sanctuary":

"Lord Prepare me to be a sanctuary, Pure and holy, tried and true. With thanksgiving, I'll be a living, Sanctuary for You."---Scruggs/Thompson, BMI

"Then the eleven disciples went away into Galilee, to the mountain which Jesus had appointed for them," (Matthew 28:16).

Jesus was leaving the earth.

He had been crucified on Calvary.

He had been resurrected from the dead.

He was victorious over all things and finishing His course.

He invited the Disciples to Mount Tabor, A Prepared Place of manifestation.

The phrase "A Prepared Place" is echoing within my heart as I write this teaching.

The School of The Holy Spirit has been marvelous. The person of the Holy Spirit has been present in full manifestation.

Needs have been met for those who sought His help and input.

"Why Was That So Easy?"

After a class I wondered, "Why was that so easy?"

Part of it was that the people in attendance wanted to be there.

The move of The Holy Spirit is in direct proportion to the hunger present.

A second is that the meetings have been conditioned with prayer. Because of this, the Holy Spirit's presence among those of us who gather together is not a new occasion.

The Holy Spirit knows He is welcome when we get together.

Because of these facts, we are able to meet in "A Prepared Place."

"When they saw Him, they worshiped Him; but some doubted," (Matthew 28:17)

Everyone present at The School of The Holy Spirit "saw Him" minister to other believers in attendance. No one doubted Him. We were all increased.

"And Jesus came and spoke to them, saying, "All authority has been given to Me in heaven and on earth." *(Matthew 28:18).*

Jesus understood His mission. He came to earth at the direction of The Father. Jesus set aside His God powers to function as a man. But, while ministering here He was not functioning in the natural. Jesus was moving in the supernatural as a man exercising spiritual authority.

"Go therefore and make disciples of all the nations, baptizing them in the name of the Father and of the Son and of the Holy Spirit," (Matthew 28:19).

My ministry has always done a remarkable job of developing disciples.

Yet, I have become better (and will become much better) at evangelism.

> *"teaching them to observe all things that I have commanded you; and lo, I am with you always, even to the end of the age." Amen." (Matthew 28:20).*

The pathway to this state is teaching.

I enjoy preaching...loud...emotional...preaching. But, I seldom get to practice the craft as it most pleases me. Teaching is not glamorous but necessary to bring believers to maturity.

Teaching is necessary...even when it becomes repetitive to the teacher.

Two Things Oral Roberts Shared About Teaching

1. *"When you are sick of saying it, they are just beginning to hear it."*

2. *"When they are sick of hearing it, they are just beginning to get it."*

Your life will be better when you choose to live it deliberately.

Directionless living leaves when it is replaced by conscious choice.

I have repeatedly experienced the power of A Prepared Place.

I plan to Prepare a Place to experience God today.

8
Not Guilty Of This One

(Todays Devotion is Taken From Psalm 14:1)

Harsh rhetoric is nothing new.

Politics has always been rough.

General Alexander Haig died in 2010.

Ramrod straight, Haig wore a size 42 long suit.

He loved pointing out the fact he could buy "off the rack."

Mr. Haig had served as Ronald Reagan's Secretary of State.

Haig was an ultra-conservative who was driven to distraction by liberals.

A holdover from the Ford Administration, General Haig also led NATO for President Jimmy Carter. The acid-tongued Haig enraged Mr. Carter when he described the new President as both "weak kneed" and "spineless."

Days after their acrimonious exchange, communist terrorists attempted to blow up the car in which Haig was riding to the base near Brussels, Belgium. Hearing of Haig's close call, President Carter had Secretary of Defense Harold Brown call and tell the General, "The President wants you to know it wasn't us."

Not one to be outdone, Haig retorted, "I knew the administration had nothing to do with the attack. It came too close to being successful."

So, you may be wondering, what has this story to do with to-day's teaching?

Nothing. I just like sharing it. But, seriously, folks...

> *"The fool has said in his heart, "There is no God," (Psalm 14:1).*

Christianity is experiential.

Ours is a faith based upon relationship.

I have never really doubted the existence of God.

I have never really doubted the existence of God because I have known Him from my early days.

Feel free to attribute this to my devout upbringing or whatever pleases you, I simply have never doubted the existence of God.

Even during the years when I strayed far from The Lord and did not honor Him with my lifestyle, I knew He was there.

He proved His eternal presence over a recent weekend during a remarkable series of meetings at The School of The Holy Spirit. The Holy Spirit was manifestly present and we were all able to draw closer to Jesus.

My consciousness of God has always been very vivid.

As I was taught early, "A man with an experience is never at the mercy of a man with an argument."

I have experienced God. Today I have no question He is alive and doing exploits. His presence is undeniably real to me.

I encourage you to press into a deeper relationship with Him than you have ever known. Don't wait. Do so today.

Declare your faith in The Lord.

Charge your atmosphere with words of faith.

I have chosen to extend myself to Him in faith...I will not regret such an act.

Extend yourself to Him.

You will not be disappointed for choosing to do so.

9
Fire On The Altar

(Today's Devotion is Taken From Leviticus 9:23-24)

Fire cleanses.

Fire warms and gives light.

The fire of God consumes the sacrifice of praise.

My heart longs for the fire of God to fall from heaven.

This fire will cleanse me of anything that dishonors God.

This fresh fire will reenergize and refocus my faith walk on Him.

This has been a week of time in the presence of God. Life is better.

Such an outpouring leaves the certain knowledge that God is involved with us.

> *"And Moses and Aaron went into the tabernacle of meeting," (Leviticus 9:23).*

Memories of Scotty Brooks

Team ministry is essential. This is true of a church or a business. Two, according to Scripture, are better than one.

Moses went into the tabernacle and ministered under the direction of Aaron.

For every Moses you must have an Aaron...someone behind the scenes making the ministry "go."

Scott Brooks was a point guard for the Houston Rockets during their glory years. He played on the team with Hakeem Olajuwon, Clyde "The Glide" Drexler, Kenny "The Jet" Smith and other outstanding basketball players. Scott was a hustling overachiever who seemed to use every bit of his ability to win. For the past few years Scott has been a head coach. No one thought him to be very good...until Kevin Durant arrived in Oklahoma City.

Then the team added Russell Westbrook and Schott went from being a good coach to being a great one. The addition of these two magnificent players caused Scott to be mentioned as a candidate for Coach of The Year.

When I saw Scott on TV I had a thought: "How many Pastors need God to send them the equivalent of a Kevin Durant and a Russell Westbrook in order to achieve their potential?"

The knowledge of winning basketball was in Scotty Brooks. It took someone with the willingness and ability to execute his plan to cause him to be recognized as an exceptional coach. How many Pastors simply need one superstar disciple who is willing to work with them toward achieving a supernatural championship? My continual prayer is that The Holy Spirit will complete the team.

> *"...and came out and blessed the people,"*
> *(Leviticus 9:23b).*

I served over 30 years as a pastor. I also have served as a Bishop, or Apostle. Still, I am prejudiced in favor of pastoral ministry.

Moses was serving, typologically, in a pastoral role as he blessed

Israel. My prayer is that each reader has a personal pastor with whom they are well acquainted.

Having someone qualified to speak the blessings of God over your life is a powerful source of encouragement.

It is also a necessary thing when confronted by the extreme challenges of life.

> *"Then the glory of the LORD appeared to all the people,"*
> *(Leviticus 9:23b)*

The manifest presence of God appeared before Israel.

This was a sign that the sacrifices offered by Moses and Aaron had been accepted by The Lord.

One of my great anticipations is the day when the glory of God is fully manifest in the local church. My heart longs for the hour when it is made apparent to the entire world---believing and unbelieving---that our sacrificial service is acceptable to Him.

> *"...and fire came out from before the LORD and consumed the burnt offering and the fat on the altar," (Leviticus 9:24)*

Remember the big "God moments" in your life.

This was a treasured time in the national life of Israel.

The Priests built fires from the fire that fell on the altar and kept them burning for hundreds of years.

They did this as a reminder that their Holy God found their sacrifice acceptable and honored them with His manifest presence.

As we celebrate the presence and power of the Holy Spirit we are, like Israel of old, continuing to keep the fire burning in our camp.

> *"When all the people saw it, they shouted and fell on their faces," (Leviticus 9:24b).*

The people rejoiced over the clearly apparent favor of God.

May the fire of God fall in each church and consume the sacrifice of praise and worship.

Our lives will be cleansed, our focus corrected, our goals clarified and, most important of all, our Lord Jesus will be glorified.

10
Self Denial

(Today's Devotion is Taken From Mark 9:49-50)

Self Denial.

Self Denial requires focused effort.

Self Denial brings victory over the flesh.

Self Denial, as you will learn, is not always about fasting.

This teaching was motivated in large part by an event that transpired on a Wednesday night in the Spring of 2010.

The need for self-denial was stirred by a homeless man who came by the church before that evening's service. He walked through the door and loudly demanded help. Prior to that Wednesday night I had never refused to help anyone in the more than 20 years I had served as Pastor of Northgate.

Before I could speak, he began cursing and making threats to kill me and burn the building.

I have been cursed before. I have had people make rude gestures before. I am not from a sheltered background, so that was not the first time I had been exposed to such language.

But, I must admit to going completely livid when the guy spat upon the church door and announced, "God does not live here!"

"For everyone will be seasoned with fire, and every sacrifice will be seasoned with salt," (Mark 9:49)

Please consider with me the type of self-denial taught by verse 49.

Refusing to retaliate during a time of provocation definitely qualifies as "denying the flesh."

Before you have the urge to rebuke me, I know my desire to attack the man was completely incorrect even if stirred by his threatening and my own simple desire for self-protection.

It would be nice (but a complete "fudge") to say God's grace quickly rose within me and I chose to defuse the situation with calm. But, if you know me at all you know that was not all there was working within me.

My prime reason for not "smacking" the man was the fact two church members arrived to the property during his tirade. No, I was not alone. In that highly agitated moment, the Holy Spirit gave me a mental image of me, their pastor, responding to violence with more of the same. It did not seem as if it would have been a good imprint.

Had I continued in the direction things were headed the event would have been "seasoned" and preserved in the memories of those who saw it...to all our detriment.

> *"Salt is good, but if the salt loses its flavor, how will you season it? Have salt in yourselves, and have peace with one another," (Mark 9:50).*

I just described denying oneself when bad behavior seems desirable. Yet, most other Bible teachers consider and write of self denial in the positive sense of a desire to grow closer to the Lord through fasting.

Before leaving for a missions trip to China my family spent the last 10 days in a focused fasting mode. Honestly, I did not enjoy it much. I wanted beef...an entire cow...and I wanted it right away!

So, no, the idea of fasting is not a scintillating one for me.

But seeing God intervene on our behalf does excite me...even more than beef. Fasting surely played a role in the move of the Holy Spirit we saw during our time of ministry in Northeast China.

Self-denial is one of the keys to living of spiritual power and supernatural demonstration.

If the church is living a life devoid of supernatural power, we are moving in a much lower level of effectiveness than our Lord desires for us.

Yeah, self-denial. Who wants it? Few of us do.

The real question is: Who needs the result?

We all need the power that self-denial releases.

11
Traditional Thinking...Wrong Again
(Today's Devotion is Based Upon Romans 16:3-6; 25-27)

Advertising interests me.

One ad reads: "Half and Half."

Another: "Fat-Free Half and Half."

My mind immediately asks, "Huh?"

Without a lot of thought, I prefer the original. When it comes to the Word of God, only the original is valid.

No, I am not about to launch some "King James is the only Bible" bit. Oh, I do have a preferred translation...*The New King James.* But translation alone does not matter nearly so much as translation and application. We can have a perfectly good translation that benefits us little unless we are willing to apply it properly. As we best comprehend, we must be faithful to the original intent of the writers.

Christianity's fear of error caused us to lean toward *orthodoxy* (right doctrine) at the expense of *orthopraxis* (right practice). But, I must quickly explain we cannot have correct practice without a proper belief system.

> *"Greet Priscilla and Aquila, my fellow workers in Christ Jesus, 4 who risked their own necks for my life, to whom not only I give thanks, but also all the churches of the Gentiles. 5 Likewise greet the church that is in their house. Greet my beloved Epaenetus, who is the firstfruits of*

Achaia to Christ. 6 Greet Mary, who labored much for us,"
(Romans 16:3-5)

A man from Conroe called me. He identified himself as a "paramedic and minister."

My guess is if he can't save lives he can bury people.

I had a daily radio program in «drive time» for a number of years. He had heard me describe God as an "equal opportunity employer." He wanted me to know he agreed that women can engage in public ministry...*but not as Pastors.*

God has never placed restrictions upon women and does not today. The well-meaning paramedic's opinion is just that...an *opinion.*

Please note that Paul greeted Priscilla, her husband Aquilla and the people of the church *they* had established *together.*

Sequence Can Be Important In Scripture.

Please note that Priscilla's name was mentioned first. Paul recognized that she and her husband were church planters---Apostles. To my understanding, an Apostle can function in any of the other five-fold ministry offices (Prophet, Evangelist, Pastor or Teacher).

> *"Greet Andronicus and Junia, my countrymen and my fellow prisoners, who are of note among the apostles, who also were in Christ before me," (Romans 16:6).*

A second substantiation of women as Apostles is found in verse seven. Prejudice against women in ministry has apparently been around since the early days of the Christian Church. As proof, some ancient manuscripts changed Junia's name to Juno in an attempt to subjugate the ministry and role women.

I find it totally distasteful that insecure men will attempt to misapply Scripture to assert some unfathomable control issue, *but they do.*

> *"Now to Him who is able to establish you according to my gospel and the preaching of Jesus Christ, according to the revelation of the mystery kept secret since the world began 26 but now made manifest, and by the prophetic Scriptures made known to all nations, according to the commandment of the everlasting God, for obedience to the faith— 27 to God, alone wise, be glory through Jesus Christ forever. Amen." (Romans 16:25-27)*

Paul prayed that God would establish us in his gospel. The gospel Paul preached was one of Divine revelation...*not history, philosophy or opinion.*

In the natural realm, I guess "Fat-Free Half and Half" beats nothing. But, nothing beats the real thing...*the pure Word of God.*

Ladies, expect to be used of God each and every day.

You have God's approval. *And mine.*

12
The Pathway To Victory

(Today's Teaching is Based On Psalm 108:1-5;7; 12-13)

I remember the question. It was a common one in my rural home church. The people would smilingly ask, "Have you got the victory?"

A successful Christian life certainly involves warfare. We are called to fight the good fight of faith. The only good fight is a fight you win. Let's look at some steps to victory:

1. Walk In Unshakeable Faith.

"O God, my heart is steadfast;" (Psalm 108:1)

Steadfast people are immovable. They cannot be moved from their posture of faith. These people know situations come and go but their God is eternal.

When you recognize no natural thing has the ability to separate you from the Lord, your life will change for the better. Your faith will become completely unshakeable.

2. Give The Lord Praise Throughout Your Waking Hours.

"I will sing and give praise, even with my glory. 2 Awake, lute and harp! I will awaken the dawn.' (Psalm 108:2).

Condition your atmosphere. Your words create environment. Faith rises or falls dependent upon words. Praise draws right spirits and repels evil spirits. Praise activates the angelic host to work in your behalf.

Praise stirs the heart of God and causes the hand of God to bring about the things you need and desire. Never lose sight of the fact your life in the Kingdom began with words and will continue as one of victory or defeat based upon words.

3. Declare The Greatness of God

"For Your mercy is great above the heavens, And Your truth reaches to the clouds. 5 Be exalted, O God, above the heavens, And Your glory above all the earth;"
(Psalm 108:4-5)

Our God is great. Our Lord is greatly to be praised. The Psalmist was demonstrating this skill.

Hell hears and fears the declared greatness of God. Those who speak by faith before they see natural results terrify hell.

4. Know That God Desires To Deliver His People

"That Your beloved may be delivered, Save with Your right hand, and hear me." (Psalm 108:6).

God is not in the business of teaching through the injection of evil. He does not bring calamity but is close to us during diffi-cult days.

The Psalmist knew that praise generated deliverance.

God's righteous right hand is working in your behalf.

Your deliverance is always His desire.

5. Recognize That The Powers Of Hell Cannot Prevail Against The Holiness Of God.

"God has spoken in His holiness: "I will rejoice;"
(Psalm 108:7).

Holiness is a force. Faith always releases more faith. The force of honor releases the force of holiness. Rejoicing simply because God has spoken guarantees victory. Our God is a Holy God. As we speak of His holiness we will find ourselves becoming more like Him: Holy!

6. Understand There Are Situations Only God Can Help.

"Give us help from trouble, For the help of man is useless"
(Psalm 108:12)

I have had times when I have felt beyond help. Honestly, there have been times when man could not help. When I was diagnosed with pancreatic cancer in 2013, man could not help...*but God could and did!*

I don't fall for this trap as often as I once did because I've come to learn to depend upon God for the miraculous. Still, this emotional set-up remains one of satan's all-time best tricks.

When individuals feel, for instance, they have "gone too far" they often are deluded into believing there is no help for them.

Please grasp this truth: *There is no situation that can move you so far that God cannot help you.*

You are never beyond the reach of our Lord. There is no sin so great He is unwilling or incapable of forgiving. There is no sickness or disease He is powerless against. Let me share this again...*God is not against you*. Our God is for you...*period*.

It's that simple

7. Continually Speak Your Expectation Of Victory.

"Through God we will do valiantly, For it is He who shall tread down our enemies," (Psalm 108:13).

My role is not to do the battle fighting. My role is to use my faith and do the believing. My mountain erodes each time I speak my expectation of victory.

Your mountain is teetering before you. Speak to it again. Tell it you expect it to fall...*and fall quickly.*

So, "Have you got the victory today?"

It is available to those who try.

13
The Lady Had Him Pegged

(Today's Devotion is Taken From Judges 4:14-24)

Pegged.

I was an adventurous child. It took me awhile to learn reality.

Obeying Granny was a hard reality. Granny would say, "I had you pegged."

It meant what I did was not surprising to her.

Our God has always used women in ministry. I do not know why we consider this a "new thing." The Prophet Deborah was a remarkably gifted woman. Barak, leader of the army of Israel, refused to fight without her. Credit Barak: He valued victory above the taunts of jealous men.

My position favoring and advocating the role of women in ministry has brought criticism to me. But, I would rather experience the criticism than see women held back for unscriptural reasons.

> *"Then Deborah said to Barak, "Up! For this is the day in which the LORD has delivered Sisera into your hand. Has not the LORD gone out before you?" So Barak went down from Mount Tabor with ten thousand men following him,"* (Judges 4:14).

Timing is critical with God. Israel did not go to war on its own. Israel moved when the Holy Spirit spoke to Deborah. In the timing of God, the powers of hell were vulnerable to attack.

We could profit from mastering such a principle today and refusing to move without His direction. Our gains would be immeasurably greater and our losses so comparatively small as to be minuscule.

> *"And the LORD routed Sisera and all his chariots and all his army with the edge of the sword before Barak; and Sisera alighted from his chariot and fled away on foot.16 But Barak pursued the chariots and the army as far as Harosheth Hagoyim, and all the army of Sisera fell by the edge of the sword; not a man was left," (Judges 4:15-16).*

God does not deal in partial victories. Our God moves in overwhelming force. Humans must count the cost before going to war. Nations must know ahead of time if they can afford the war. For believers, our God is so great there is no cost to consider.

There is only overwhelming victory to anticipate.

> *"However, Sisera had fled away on foot to the tent of Jael, the wife of Heber the Kenite; for there was peace between Jabin king of Hazor and the house of Heber the Kenite," (Judges 4:17).*

Sisera was a vaunted Canaanite warrior. Legend says animals died at the sound of his voice. Walls were said to fall before the power of his shouted commands. General Sisera may have been guilty of reading his own press releases. I have done business with nationally known ministers who write and believe their own press releases. Trouble has often followed them.

In the case of Sisera, a supernatural surprise was in the offing for him.

Shockingly overwhelmed by Holy Spirit empowered Israel, Sisera fled to the home of an Israeli friend.

"And Jael went out to meet Sisera, and said to him, "Turn aside, my lord, turn aside to me; do not fear." And when he had turned aside with her into the tent, she covered him with a blanket," (Judges 4:18).

Jael, the wife of Heber, went out to greet Sisera. Totally against protocol, she invited him into her family tent. Even more out of bounds, she consoled and covered him with a blanket.

"Then he said to her, "Please give me a little water to drink, for I am thirsty." So she opened a jug of milk, gave him a drink, and covered him," (Judges 4:19)

Sisera was apparently accustomed to finding "favor" with women. He asked Jael for some water and sacked out. Life probably seemed better to him.

"And he said to her, "Stand at the door of the tent, and if any man comes and inquires of you, and says, 'Is there any man here?' you shall say, 'No.'" (Judges 4:20).

Using people comes easily for some folks. I am concerned about our depersonalized society. I see people talking on cell-phones while waiters attempt to serve them. Each time you do so you are declaring that individual is not a person of value, but something to be used.

Sisera was clearly a "user". Valuing his own safety above Jael's reputation, Sisera instructed her to lie if anyone asked of his whereabouts.

"Then Jael, Heber's wife, took a tent peg and took a hammer in her hand, and went softly to him and drove the peg into his temple, and it went down into the ground; for he was fast asleep and weary. So he died." (Judges 4:21)

Arrogant Sisera fell into a deep sleep. Jael took a tent peg and drove it through Sisera's head. She hit the peg with such force that the anchoring device entered the soil beneath the tent.

The Bible is filled with understatement, but few statements exceed this one... "So he died." Please pardon my Southernism but, "I guess so!"

> *"And then, as Barak pursued Sisera, Jael came out to meet him, and said to him, "Come, I will show you the man whom you seek." And when he went into her tent, there lay Sisera, dead with the peg in his temple," (Judges 4:22).*

Jael caught the attention of Barak and offered to lead him to Sisera. Imagine the surprise of Barak as he found the Canaanite Captain nailed to the floor of the tent. To amplify on a New Testament thought, not only will your sins "find you out," they will "nail you."

> *"So on that day God subdued Jabin king of Canaan in the presence of the children of Israel. 24 And the hand of the children of Israel grew stronger and stronger against Jabin king of Canaan, until they had destroyed Jabin king of Canaan," (Judges 4:23-24).*

The New Testament principle here is one of power over demonic spirits. When the strong man is taken down the people of God are free to do the work of the Lord. Move in the Name of Jesus to defeat the adversaries surrounding you and your family today.

Your victory is an absolute certainty.

14
Shouting Praises Until The Transition
(Today's Devotion is Taken From Psalm 98:1-4)

I've seen enough death.

Yes, I know I will see my loved ones again. That thought alone is enough to keep me going forward. When we understand what really lies ahead we can remain positive.

My faith is intact and my expectation of better days is stronger than ever. My trust is not in things that originate in earth but those drawn from the heavenly realm

> *"Oh, sing to the Lord a new song! For He has done marvelous things; His right hand and His holy arm have gained Him the victory," (Psalm 98:1)*

I am a praiser. I love up-tempo praise music. But I thrive on the intensity of worship. Still, praise and worship are not really about music. Clearly music can be used to bring these acts into manifestation.

But praise and worship are both deliberate actions of the will of man.

During difficult days we must choose to go deeper with God.

> *"The Lord has made known His salvation; His righteousness He has revealed in the sight of the nations. 3 He has remembered His mercy and His faithfulness to the house of Israel; All the ends of the earth have seen the salvation of our God," (Psalm 98:2-3)*

God is a promise keeper. People routinely keep promises. Others try but fail to keep their word. Most fail because they simply cannot do so. Far too many others fail because of flawed integrity.

Our Lord not only wants to keep His promises...*He does keep them!*

> *"Shout joyfully to the Lord, all the earth; Break forth in song, rejoice, and sing praises," (Psalm 98:4).*

Dr. Ron Smith was my spiritual father. I spent much of the last week of "Papa Ron's" life by his bedside. Throughout my visits with him I would alternately sing, preach and pray.

He would often let loose a shout of praise that caused the hospital staff to come to him. With a glowing face and uplifted hands he would tell them, "No, I'm not in pain. I'm just praising my Lord!"

One of my life determinations is that I will finish the course strong.

No, I'm not one of those who is longing for heaven. My longing is to succeed in the work of God here. I will not go off to heaven with a whimper. My plan is to go out with a shout!

Just like my Papa Ron.

15
Minimum Standard Christianity
(Today's Teaching is Taken From Luke 6:46-48)

Salvation is a simple process: Call upon the Name of Jesus and be saved.

The effective Christian life is a bit more complicated. We are living during a time of record conversions to Christianity. Sadly, we are also living during a time of very low standards for Christian believers. Yes, immature Christian believers will still go to heaven.

They just won't take many folks with them.

> *"But why do you call Me 'Lord, Lord,' and not do the things which I say?" (Luke 6:46).*

Jesus is not pleased by the ignorance of His church. We are not saved by works. But, the saved should work.

Salvation is a supernatural event. The saved should strive to be like Jesus. Jesus gave everything; He shed His blood. His flesh was literally ripped from His body.

Jesus is Savior. I have no doubt of that. But how many believers fervently pursue Him as Lord?

His question still rings true today, "How can we really call Him Lord without doing what He says?"

> *"Whoever comes to Me, and hears My sayings and does them, I will show you whom he is like:" (Luke 6:47).*

Being born again is enough to go to heaven. But, we must grow in the things of God in order to mature. Those who come to God and learn His Word are established in the faith. Those established in the faith can live out the example of the type believer Jesus desires that we all be.

> *"He is like a man building a house, who dug deep and laid the foundation on the rock. And when the flood arose, the stream beat vehemently against that house, and could not shake it, for it was founded on the rock," (Luke 6:48).*

Storms come to every life. Effective preparation must be made before the storm. Many die prematurely because they do not study healing until they are sick.

Studying prosperity principles en route to the bankruptcy court is probably a bit late.

Those who study the Word and make a conscious effort to live it are described in this verse. These are the people who dig deep into the things of God in order to establish their foundation.

Legendary minister Derek Prince told an amazing tale of a five-story home he owned in Jerusalem. The house had been built on a small piece of land purchased by a growing family that continually built extra floors to accommodate the new additions to the family. One day Brother Prince came home to his wife, Lydia, and the 10 children they had adopted...*to find the house leaning to one side.*

> *"But he who heard and did nothing is like a man who built a house on the earth without a foundation, against which the stream beat vehemently; and immediately it fell. And the ruin of that house was great," (Luke 6:49).*

Not all storms are dramatic events. Some problems develop through the typical pressures of life. You have probably guessed the source of the problem for the Prince home. It was not built upon an established foundation. It was erected directly upon concrete blocks that sat atop raw earth.

As the extra floors were built onto the home the blocks on one side of the structure began to be pressed downward into the unstabilized soil.

Thankfully, the home was saved with some extreme foundation repair in the form of piers drilled down to a layer of rock.

If you are alive and breathing it is not too late to work on your foundation. Dig deep into the Word of God for bedrock truths upon which to build your life.

Reading through the Bible on a daily basis is one of the most foundational things you can do to enhance your life in the Kingdom.

16
A Day Spent Trying To Touch Bottom
(Today's Devotion is Taken From Psalm 69:1-3; 13-14)

Yes, I was a sneaky kid.

People would have been surprised. I pretended to be the model "church kid." But, I was strong-willed and "set" on having my way. I often managed to "fake out" my Mom because I was non-confrontational.

Perception is an amazing thing. One of my younger brothers was actually into less wrong-doing than me. But, it was not apparent because he was so publicly disobedient and openly confrontational with our parents.

> *"Save me, O God! For the waters have come up to my neck,"*
> *(Psalm 69:1).*

On a particularly hot Summer day, I wanted to go swimming. Mom did not have a lot of rules but swimming alone was a non-negotiable on her list of "no no's." Knowing this, I simply walked down to the East Fork of the San Jacinto River without bothering to ask permission.

Enjoying the cool waters, I swam in the shallows for awhile but became more adventurous and "dog paddled" out into the main channel of the sandy brown colored, slow moving stream.

> *"I sink in deep mire, Where there is no standing; I have*
> *come into deep waters, Where the floods overflow me,"*
> *(Psalm 69:2).*

Much to my surprise, I tired and had a hard time getting back to shore. The horrible realization hit me: *I could not touch bottom!*

Being alone intensified the fear.

> *"I am weary with my crying; My throat is dry; My eyes fail while I wait for my God," (Psalm 69:3).*

I have had a few instances of futilely searching for the bottom. I know what it is like to have spent a lot of hours swimming in deep water and becoming tired out. I have not necessarily cried a lot. But I know what it is like to have my eyes literally ache from extreme concentration.

When Granny Hewlett, a dear church member, went to heaven, her devout daughter spoke of *"...trying to find the bottom of the pool."*

She obviously comes from a higher social station than a self-described "River Rat" from Plum Grove, Texas. Still the dilemma remains the same and demands to be answered: *"What do I need to do when I'm sinking?"*

> *"But as for me, my prayer is to You, O LORD, in the acceptable time; O God, in the multitude of Your mercy, Hear me in the truth of Your salvation," (Psalm 69:13).*

Each answer has a commonality. The answer always involves looking to Him. Our tough days are no different than other days to God. The acceptable time for Him to act during the era of grace in which we live today is the moment when we believe.

My faith is set. Nothing "out there" has the power to consume me. I believe God's will for my life is good. His plan is for my life is perfect. Therefore, I have already won.

"Deliver me out of the mire, And let me not sink; Let me be delivered from those who hate me, And out of the deep waters." (Psalm 69:14).

No one is "hating on me." But I have been in over my head. Our God will not let you or me sink. We are all coming out of the deep waters. His promise remains, "Our future will be better than our past."

We will not drown. We won't even go under.

17
Obedient To The Heavenly Vision?
(Today's Teaching is Taken From Acts 26:19-25)

The greatness of God is obvious. His Majesty is there to be experienced. The fact He has a plan for people still amazes me.

I am awed by His obvious affection for imperfect humanity. I am not a perfect guy. I still have struggles, both spiritual and natural...*just like everyone else*. But years of sanctification have brought me to the place of living my life in consistent obedience.

> *"Therefore, King Agrippa, I was not disobedient to the heavenly vision," (Acts 26:19),*

Paul was as human as anyone who ever lived on planet earth. His struggle against intellectual pride and educational arrogance was clearly a lifelong battle. However, there is one thing Paul cannot be charged with: *disobedience to the will of God for his life.* Going even deeper, I do not see a single instance where Paul was indifferent to the desires and direction of The Holy Spirit.

In my own life, indifference, most often in the form of selfishness, has been my consistent undoing.

> *"but declared first to those in Damascus and in Jerusalem, and throughout all the region of Judea, and then to the Gentiles, that they should repent, turn to God, and do works befitting repentance," (Acts 26:20).*

The example of Paul's life is a useful one. Immediately upon conversion he witnessed to those around him. As he developed in faith and grew in ministry skill, Paul ministered wherever the

Holy Spirit opened doors for him.

If the people who work around you don't know you're a Christian, something is wrong with your personal code of conduct.

> *"For these reasons the Jews seized me in the temple and tried to kill me . 22 Therefore, having obtained help from God, to this day I stand, witnessing both to small and great, saying no other things than those which the prophets and Moses said would come— 23 that the Christ would suffer, that He would be the first to rise from the dead, and would proclaim light to the Jewish people and to the Gentiles,"* (Acts 26:21-23).

Some years ago I read a self-help book called *"Who Moved My Cheese?"* Two things happened everywhere Paul traveled: *a riot or a revival.* In some cases, a revival was preceded or followed by a riot. Paul didn't mind moving the cheese wheel of his disciples.

> *"Now as he thus made his defense, Festus said with a loud voice, "Paul, you are beside yourself! Much learning is driving you mad!" (Acts 26:24).*

Paul was a person of *renown* before his conversion. He continued to be a person of public *interest* thereafter. On trial for his life, Paul so effectively represented the spiritual changes in his life that he was accused of being mentally ill.

Some years ago I had a similar conversation with one of my brothers. He could not understand my perseverance in the face of bad news. Actually, I was facing something beyond bad news. It was a cancer diagnosis that was more like "impending doom." But, my faith was set for victory, a fact that was amazing to my brother.

His response was much like that of King Festus to Paul. "Big

Brother, you have read that Bible so much it has made you crazy,» he said. «You have lost touch with reality.»

Actually, like Paul, I had found reality...*faith in the Word of God.* Faith in the Word of God is the reality that has enriched my life.

The thing I was believing for, my healing, came into being and drew my brother toward the Lord. God always desires to bring something good out of the bad things we face.

> *"But he said, "I am not mad, most noble Festus, but speak the words of truth and reason," (Acts 26:25).*

Today, like many who read this, I have faced challenges. I have had to realize the need to "see" myself completely healed.

When I "saw" myself well, visionary faith began to work within my spirit and healing followed my faith.

I still have a challenge, but, like the Apostle Paul, my faith is set and I am moving forward.

The God who brought me great victories in days past will do so again.

What God has done for you He will do again!

18
Living Stones or Memorial Stones?
(Today's Teaching is Taken From Acts 1:4-8; 2:1-4)

The church in the United States is in an interesting place. We live in a season when mega churches abound throughout the land. Yet, more pastors leave the ministry than enter and we see a continuing decade-long trend of more churches closing than opening.

My question for all believers everywhere is a simple two-fold one, "Are we to be a memorial to things past? Or, should we be living stones building up the House of God today?"

One of the things burning within me is the need to start and continue "right." If the church was started by a display of the power of God, should not the church continue to be a place where the power of God is displayed?

We make a distinction that God never desired. We describe some churches as Spirit-filled and others as not. God never desired such a distinction to be made because all believers in the early church were Spirit-filled.

Some reading this today may ask "What does he mean by using the term ‹Spirit-filled?"

We are describing those born again believers who have received Spirit-Baptism.

While I know this is not a theological position to which all churches hold, I believe it to be the Biblical standard. It is the position of the church I pastored for 20-plus years, and it is the posture of the churches with which I associate today.

The initial evidence of Spirit-Baptism is speaking in a language unknown to the speaker. Said in the language of the day, "speaking in tongues."

We are still being falsely accused of teaching that people must "speak in tongues" in order to be saved. We do not believe, and never have believed, such a bad and potentially destructive doctrine.

Let me share some facts that will keep the church alive and moving as an example of what God desires to do rather than being a memorial to what has already taken place.

Spirit-Baptism is The Promise of The Father

We, like the disciples of old, are commanded to seek the "Promise of The Father."

> 4 And being assembled together with them, He commanded them not to depart from Jerusalem, but to wait for the Promise of the Father, "which," He said, "you have heard from Me; 5 for John truly baptized with water, but you shall be baptized with the Holy Spirit not many days from now." 6 Therefore, when they had come together, they asked Him, saying, "Lord, will You at this time restore the kingdom to Israel?" 7 And He said to them, "It is not for you to know times or seasons which the Father has put in His own authority. 8 But you shall receive power when the Holy Spirit has come upon you; and you shall be witnesses to Me in Jerusalem, and in all Judea and Samaria, and to the end of the earth," (Acts 1:4-8).

God is always moving His people into a deeper relationship with Him (vs 5).

Someone will always object to the move of God in your life (vs 6).

God always clarifies the thought process of those who really desire such (vs 7).

God always wants to empower us to witness for Jesus.

Spirit Baptism Is An Experience That Opens The Supernatural Realm

"When the Day of Pentecost had fully come, they were all with one accord in one place. 2 And suddenly there came a sound from heaven, as of a rushing mighty wind, and it filled the whole house where they were sitting. 3 Then there appeared to them divided tongues, as of fire, and one sat upon each of them. 4 And they were all filled with the Holy Spirit and began to speak with other tongues, as the Spirit gave them utterance," (Acts 2:1-4).

God has always moved and done things in particular seasons (1A).

Unity is essential. Unity is not an option. I understand and desire this more than ever (1B).

The Full-Gospel Church has a particular sound (2). That sound was initially described as a "rushing mighty wind", symbolic of God's urgent desire to meet the needs of His people.

We are the spiritual house where God dwells. God desires to fill the "whole house" with His power and glory.

As we walk with our Lord, the fire of God's holiness falls upon us in a sanctifying way. It is through this we come to understand the critical importance of His being number one.

What is the proof of Holy Spirit's activity? James calls the tongue the most unruly member of the body. Giving your tongue over to God for His glory is proof of a supernatural experience with Him.

Spirit Baptism Evokes An Eternal Question

"12 So they were all amazed and perplexed, saying to one another, "Whatever could this mean?" 13 Others mocking said, "They are full of new wine."

I have no problem with those who ask, "What is this about?" However, I will not waste time on conversation with disrespectful people bound by a spirit of religion.

Clarify What Spirit Baptism Is Really "For."

"8 But you shall receive power when the Holy Spirit has come upon you; and you shall be witnesses to Me in Jerusalem, and in all Judea and Samaria, and to the end of the earth,"(Acts 1:4-8).

The point of receiving Spirit Baptism is receiving the power of God. We are to be actively involved in ministering miracles to those who are in need of them.

R.W. Schambach told of hearing T.L. Osborn make a life-changing statement, "Those who cannot demonstrate the power of the Gospel have no right to preach the Gospel."

Words are not enough. We cannot just say we believe in the supernatural. We are to be a people of signs, wonders and miracles. Our lifestyle must be one that demonstrates the ability of God.

The choice is ours...be a Memorial Stone of what has taken place... or...be an example of what God is doing on the earth today.

19
Relationship Thoughts
(Today's Devotion is Taken From Proverbs 3:1-6)

She is a manager at one of my favorite restaurants.

I won't name her because of the confidential nature of our conversation. I love the entire Pappas Brothers Restaurant chain but The Pappadeaux Cajun Restaurant is a personal favorite. A pastor friend took me to Pappadeaux for a birthday celebration. The food was great and the interaction with the staff made the time even better.

I live by the theory that I am the "Pastor" of an area. I serve both the saved and those who are unsaved. No, I'm not the only Pastor in the area, but one of the Pastors set in office to do marketplace ministry.

Because of this motivation, it was while out with my friend that a series of conversations was started with the manager that still rings inside me. Having seen me interact with my adult children while visiting the restaurant, the manager sought me out for my opinions on parenting.

A little humor often helps open the door to conversation. So, I shared:

Five Things My Father NEVER Said

1) "Your Mom and I are going out of town for the weekend. Why don't you invite some friends over for a party?

2) Of course I would like to co-sign for you on a Corvette!

3) You cannot continue to live under my roof unless you get a tattoo.

4) Sure you can find a girl anyone would want to marry in a place like that.

5) You don't have enough money for earrings? Here's another $100...*get your nose pierced, too!"*

I am thankful for my Dad. I am even thankful I am a Dad. Yes, life has challenges aplenty. But the joy of relationship makes it all better.

Seven Relationship Related Truths
1) Learn And Remember The Word of God

"My son, do not forget my law," (Proverbs 3:1).

Relationships are the joy of my life. Relationships are also the greatest challenge of my life. Relationships can only be maximized as they are ordered in the light of the Word of God. In verse one the Holy Spirit is giving us a big insight into maintaining a successful relationship with Father God: "...remember the Word!"

2) Let The Word Of God Keep Your Heart

"But let your heart keep my commands;" (Proverbs 3:1b)

Life has a rhythm to it. Much can be learned from observing this rhythm. This is especially true in regard to the rhythm of relationships. Yet, this rhythmic cycle can also be a disruptive force in relationships.

As important as relationships are they can never be allowed to become a substitute for the Word of God. Relationships contain an ebb and flow element that can only be counteracted by the constancy of the Word of God.

3) Reap The Reward Of Obedience

"For length of days and long life and peace they will add to you," (Proverbs 3:2).

Please say this aloud where you are, *"The Word of God is a life-giver."*

Stress is a joy-robbing thief that can shorten the lives of those who do not learn how to manage it. Please do yourself a favor by declaring these words aloud, too, *"The Word of God releases the peace necessary to lengthen my life-span."*

4) Be Merciful...*Even With Those Who Don't Deserve Such*

"Let not mercy and truth forsake you; Bind them around your neck, write them on the tablet of your heart," (Proverbs 3:3).

I make the choice to live in mercy today. I will not forsake the principle that one who has been forgiven much is required to forgive much. I have been forgiven "much" and choose to freely recall this principle because it is written within the confines of my heart.

5) Live In The Favor Brought About By Obeying The Word Of God.

"And so find favor and high esteem In the sight of God and man," (Proverbs 3:4).

Honor is an incredible force. God honors us as we honor Him. The release of this favor also releases honor. Supernatural favor is released as we obey God's Word.

6) Place The Totality Of Your Trust In The Right Person.

"Trust in the LORD with all your heart, And lean not on your own understanding;" (Proverbs 3:5)

People will disappoint you. Even spiritually devout folk will fail. But, this is no reason to routinely cast people aside each time they fail in your relationship with them.

Choose to forgive and believe God will move your relationship on into better things. Choose to be a minister of reconciliation and restoration.

7) Acknowledge The Goodness Of God Each Time It Manifests.

"In all your ways acknowledge Him, And He shall direct your paths," (Proverbs 3:6).

God desires to guide His people into good things. More good things are released each time we acknowledge God's blessings.

My prayer is that you enjoy this as the special day God made for you.

20
Inescapable Truths
(This Devotion is Taken From Proverbs 15:1-4; 26; 33)

A great man sent me an email. He was pondering the hard-hitting nature of Proverbs. I understand his reaction to this Old Testament Book of Wisdom. Proverbs illustrates life through spiritual truth that is often contrasted with absurdity.

I am not speaking for my friend, but I have had days when my own absurdity was obviously apparent. Yes, I have happily found myself in Proverbs. But, I have also been depressed to find myself described in Proverbs when I was identified by inescapable truth.

> *"A soft answer turns away wrath, But a harsh word stirs up anger," (Proverbs 15:1).*

I love soft words. But, I struggle with this one. Aggressive speech provokes me. My first instinct is to respond sharply.

I exert much effort toward not disrespecting others. I had an opportunity to practice this principle early yesterday. Candidly, disrespect angers me like nothing else on the planet. Disrespect was directed my way and I wanted to verbally hammer the offender. But, the Holy Spirit was present to help...although my tongue is now scarred from my having bitten it.

> *"The tongue of the wise uses knowledge rightly, But the mouth of fools pours forth foolishness," (Proverbs 15:2).*

My "bestie" shared a story that made me laugh aloud. She hails from a small oilfield town located in far North Texas. My friend possesses a level of sophistication I do not have. My only "taste" seems to be in my mouth.

She read to me an e-mail from a friend of hers who had returned from New York City having just watched the play *Cats*. The premise of the long-running Broadway musical totally escaped her friend who did not grasp that the cats were symbolic of people.

I have learned the hard way that no one really knows how goofy my thoughts are...*unless I open my mouth and reveal them to all around me.*

Her friend opened her mouth, "They had those cats behaving like they were people. They were singing, dancing, falling in love, being sad, everything!"

> *"The eyes of the LORD are in every place, Keeping watch on the evil and the good," (Proverbs 15:3).*

I grew up with a lot of legalism. "An all-seeing Eye is watching you," we morbidly sang in Plum Grove. The reminder that God was watching was almost always contextualized as a negative thing. Ponder this: *God is also recording the good things you do and measuring you for a blessing.*

> *"A wholesome tongue is a tree of life, But perverseness in it breaks the spirit," (Proverbs 15:4).*

Our tongue was formed that we might praise our God. Legend declares the slave merchants who were re-selling Joseph said he had *"...a tongue that had only been used to utter praises to the Hebrew God."*

How good would life be if this could be said of us?

> *"The thoughts of the wicked are an abomination to the LORD, But the words of the pure are pleasant," (Proverbs 15:26).*

No, we don't go to hell for evil thoughts. But, our reward on earth is diminished by them. Why? Evil thinking eventually becomes evil action.

> *"The fear of the LORD is the instruction of wisdom, And before honor is humility," (Proverbs 15:33).*

Humility precedes honor. How often we reverse this paradigm! Human nature is such that we desire honor before it is earned. The pathway to blessing is plain to those seeking to walk there upon. Submission to the plan of God is the ultimate form of humility.

When we move in humility we are destined to be honored.

21
A Gross Start And A Miraculous Conclusion

(Today's Teaching is Taken From John 9:13-34)

The man had enough problems. He had been born blind...*and still was.* He sought out Jesus for healing...*and Jesus healed him.*

The way Jesus did it was a bit gross. He spat into clay and smeared it in the man's eyes. Then He told the man to walk to the Pool of Siloam and wash the clay from his formerly blind eyes.

> *13 They brought him who formerly was blind to the Pharisees. 14 Now it was a Sabbath when Jesus made the clay and opened his eyes. 15 Then the Pharisees also asked him again how he had received his sight. He said to them, "He put clay on my eyes, and I washed, and I see." 16 Therefore some of the Pharisees said, "This Man is not from God, because He does not keep the Sabbath." Others said, "How can a man who is a sinner do such signs?" And there was a division among them," (John 9:13-16)*

Religion loves the status quo. Religion seldom desires or appreciates miracles. Instead of rejoicing with the man, the Pharisees were upset because Jesus healed him on the Sabbath.

> *17 They said to the blind man again, "What do you say about Him because He opened your eyes?" He said, "He is a prophet," (John 9:17)*

The critics asked the formerly blind man his opinion of Jesus.

As you can guess, it was quite high. He correctly declared Jesus a prophet.

> *18 But the Jews did not believe concerning him, that he had been blind and received his sight, until they called the parents of him who had received his sight. 19 And they asked them, saying, "Is this your son, who you say was born blind? How then does he now see?" (John 9:18-19).*

Still looking for someone to speak against Jesus, the Pharisees began to question the man's parents. Their question indicates they suspected a hoax.

> *20 His parents answered them and said, "We know that this is our son, and that he was born blind; 21 but by what means he now sees we do not know, or who opened his eyes we do not know. He is of age; ask him. He will speak for himself." 22 His parents said these things because they feared the Jews, for the Jews had agreed already that if anyone confessed that He was Christ, he would be put out of the synagogue. 23 Therefore his parents said, "He is of age; ask him," (John 9:20-23).*

I can imagine his aged parents cowering before the Pharisees. As religious Jews, they knew the Sanhedrin Council had the power to excommunicate them. They did declare the man was their son, he had been born blind, and had been to that day.

> *24 So they again called the man who was blind, and said to him, "Give God the glory! But, as the pressure intensified, the parents "caved in" and said, "He is a grown man. He can speak for himself," (John 9:24).*

"We know that this Man is a sinner."

Their frustration mounting, the Pharisees intensified their attack.

It rankles me to read the words, *"Glorify God...not this sinner!"*

25 He answered and said, "Whether He is a sinner or not I
do not know. One thing I know: that though I was blind,
now I see," (John 9:25).

What a marvelous response. The man honestly did not know
much about Jesus. He did not know if Jesus was a sinner or a
person of reputation. But he did know something of incredible
importance to him: He was blind but now he could see.

26 Then they said to him again, "What did He do to you?
How did He open your eyes?" (John 9:26).

Picture the beautifully robed Pharisees screaming, "What kind
of trick did He pull?"

27 He answered them, "I told you already, and you did not
listen. Why do you want to hear it again? Do you also want
to become His disciples?" (John 9:27).

The restored individual had enough. It was his time to blow off
some steam.

"I have answered your questions, but you won't listen."

"Why are you guys so interested in this man? Do you want to
be His disciples?"

28 Then they reviled him and said, "You are His disciple,
but we are Moses' disciples. 29 We know that God spoke
to Moses; as for this fellow, we do not know where He is
from." (John 9:28-29)

 Angrily, the Pharisees retorted, "We are *Moses'* disciples! We
know good and well that God Almighty spoke to Moses."

"We don't know what voice this Jesus guy is claiming to hear. We don't even know where He is from!"

Four Astonishing Conclusions Spoken By The Miracle Recipient

1) It is Even More Amazing That an Unknown Man Could Work a Miracle

"The man answered and said to them, "Why, this is a marvelous thing, that you do not know where He is from; yet He has opened my eyes!" (John 9:30).

2) God Hears the Faith-filled Prayers of His People

"Now we know that God does not hear sinners; but if anyone is a worshiper of God and does His will, He hears him," (John 9:31).

3) Never Before Had the Eyes Of a Man Born Blind Been Opened

"Since the world began it has been unheard of that anyone opened the eyes of one who was born blind," (John 9:32).

4) Miracles Can Only Flow From God
"If this Man were not from God, He could do nothing."

34 They answered and said to him, "You were completely born in sins, and are you teaching us?" And they cast him out," (John 9:33-34).

Try as he might, the man could not get through to his tormentors. They declared him a sinner and excommunicated him from the Temple. As painful as that must have been, the man did not have long to wait...*the church age was at hand!*

22
A Fact Too Obvious To Ignore
(Today's Devotion is Based Upon John 8:31-36)

1522 times.

The word "if" appears in Scripture 1522 times. The vast majority of times "if" connects a requirement with a promise.

> *"Then Jesus said to those Jews who believed Him, "If you abide in My word, you are My disciples indeed," John 8:31).*

This verse proves our relationship with Jesus is conditional. Living in obedience to the Word of God proves we are His disciples. You are fulfilling one of His requirements today as you study His Word. As we learn His Word we find ourselves led into other areas of obedience.

> *"And you shall know the truth, and the truth shall make you free," (John 8:32).*

The Word of God is truth. Pontius Pilate asked Jesus, "What is truth?"

Pilate was looking into the eyes of truth... *Jesus, the Word of God come to earth in the flesh.*

We must be like Jesus. When Jesus came to earth He lived as a human---depending upon The Word and The Holy Spirit. God keeps impressing me with the need to start right in order to continue correctly.

If you need one, it is not too late for you to get a fresh start.

"They answered Him, "We are Abraham's descendants, and have never been in bondage to anyone. How can You say, 'You will be made free'?" (John 8:33).

This verse illustrates the difference between religion and relationship. Religion is a set of rules and regulations about God. Relationship is living in covenant with Him.

"Jesus answered them, "Most assuredly, I say to you, whoever commits sin is a slave of sin," (John 8:34).

Sin carries with it a price. The price for salvation was paid by Jesus. The believer who continues in sin learns sin still has a price. Jesus will not have to pay the price for sin again...*once was eternally enough.*

When we turn our backs on our Lord we find ourselves in a situation where we pay for sin through suffering.

"And a slave does not abide in the house forever, but a son abides forever," (John 8;35).

A household slave lived inside...*so long as he was productive.*

The believer---*a love slave to Jesus*---can live in the House of God forever.

"Therefore if the Son makes you free, you shall be free indeed," (John 8:36).

We belong to God through spiritual adoption. Roman law allowed the oldest son to adopt brothers.

Greek law stated that all slaves born in the House became family members.

Jesus adopted us. We, spiritual slaves, were born again in The House of God.

I will say and write this phrase throughout my lifetime:

"You are as free as you choose to be!"

You've already taken a step toward living in freedom by reading this devotion. Ask the Holy Spirit to reveal what is next on His agenda for your life.

If you do so you will not regret it for a single second.

23
Seven Facts About Jesus
(Today's Teaching is Taken From John 1:1-13)

He is the Way to Salvation. He is the Perfect Price of Salvation. He is Jesus, our Savior and our Lord.

1) Jesus Was Not Created But Has Always Existed.

"In the beginning was the Word," (John 1:1),

Jesus existed in the dateless past. He was present before the creation of the universe. He existed in the spirit realm from before the creation of time.

2) Jesus Is One Third Of The Holy Trinity

"...and the Word was with God, and the Word was God. 2 He was in the beginning with God," (John 1:1b-2).

Jesus, God The Father and The Holy Spirit make up The Holy Trinity. These three compose what scholars refer to as The Godhead. This is the fountain of salvation and the foundation of life.

3) Jesus Was Active During The Creation Event.

"All things were made through Him, and without Him nothing was made that was made," (John 1:3).

Jesus and The Holy Spirit carry out the plan of the Father. All things were made *THROUGH* Jesus *BY* The Holy Spirit. This reflects the pattern of salvation that came *THROUGH* Jesus *BY* The Holy Spirit.

4) He Is The Life And Light Of God For Those Who Believe.

"In Him was life, and the life was the light of men,"
(John 1:4).

The Holy Spirit is still doing the work of Jesus on the earth. He is leading mankind to salvation and carrying out the healing work of Jesus. The redemptive work of Jesus gives the Holy Spirit a basis point from which to work.

5) Dark Forces Could Not Defeat His Greatness.

"And the light shines in the darkness, and the darkness did not comprehend it," (John 1:5).

The satanic realm is well aware of *Who* Jesus Is. Yet, even in their intense hatred of Him, they could not comprehend a way to defeat Him. Every plan satan had for the enslavement of mankind was defeated when Jesus rose from the grave.

6) Jesus Sent Men And Women To Witness Of His Life Changing Ability.

"There was a man sent from God, whose name was John. 7 This man came for a witness, to bear witness

of the Light, that all through him might believe. 8 He
was not that Light, but was sent to bear witness of that
Light. 9 That was the true Light which gives light to every
man coming into the world," (John 1:6-9).

John The Baptist was a remarkable man. Imagine His predicament: Things changed for John the moment He introduced Jesus. He went from being the most famous preacher in Israel to not even being the best preacher in his own family.

7) Even Though Many Did Not Receive Him, We Did.

"He was in the world, and the world was made through
Him, and the world did not know Him. 11 He came to His
own, and His own did not receive Him. 12 But as many as
received Him, to them He gave the right to become children
of God, to those who believe in His name:13 who were born,
not of blood, nor of the will of the flesh, nor of the will of
man, but of God," (John 1:12B-13).

We were not born into the Royal Family. We were *born again* into the Royal Family. The moment we believed we became His own people.

I am thankful He is mine and I am His...*forever.*

24
Recovering It All

(Today's Teaching is Taken From 1 Samuel 30:1-25)

David was in a rough spot. He had been granted political asylum in the badlands. Through no fault of his own, David had fallen into disfavor with King Saul and was fleeing for his life.

David was living in *Ziklag.* The original meaning was "fortress on the slopes leading to the lower place."

The local people had changed the meaning of Ziklag to *"The Place of Utter Despair."* Can we agree that David was in a rough spot? Bad news: *It was about to get worse.*

David And His Men Had Lost It All

"David and his men reached Ziklag on the third day. Now the Amalekites had raided the Negev and Ziklag. They had attacked Ziklag and burned it, 2 and had taken captive the women and everyone else in it, both young and old. They killed none of them, but carried them off as they went on their way. 3 When David and his men reached Ziklag, they found it destroyed by fire and their wives and sons and daughters taken captive," (1Samuel 30:1-3).

The village had been burned. Entire families had been taken-captive. What possessions they owned had been looted.

They Were In A Heartbroken State

"So David and his men wept aloud until they had no strength left to weep," (Vs 4).

What a picture! Hardened men...*broken by life.* I understand this level of weeping. When my Mom died I cried until I had no ability to cry. Such is indicative of a place of emotional emptiness, like the Israeli's at Ziklag.

David Was Suffering, Too

"David's two wives had been captured—Ahinoam of Jezreel and Abigail, the widow of Nabal of Carmel," (Vs 5).

Everyone remembers David and Bathsheba, but there was another. David's great love, Abigail, had been taken captive by the Amelekites. One of King David's political wives, Ahinoam, had been kidnapped, too.

Amalek is a type of sinful flesh. It is conniving, treacherous and deadly, just like the people Israel was facing.

People Often Turn On Leadership During Rough Times

"Now David was greatly distressed, for the people spoke of stoning him, because the soul of all the people was grieved, every man for his sons and his daughters," (Vs 6a).

I have "bitten" the messenger. I have "been bitten" for being the messenger. I refuse to hide behind "truisms." The Word of God is not just what God says. The Word of God is what I believe. I will not apologize for being a man of faith.

There have been numerous times when I have been attacked as a result of standing for and promoting the Word of God. Such activity is nothing new, as we can see here.

David Made A Critically Important Right Choice

"But David strengthened himself in the Lord his God,"
(vs 6b)

Body blows come to us all. Strengthening ourselves can take on many different forms. For instance, recently I had to repent... *again*...before sharing the Word. Not because I had done something wrong. Because I had embraced hurt feelings.

I have repeatedly entertained a bad attitude over hurt feelings... *Call it "Amalek of the mind."*

David knew the loss of the woman he loved had injected broken focus into his life. He had to regain his focus and stir his faith to believe again. Our strength is always in the Lord. My prayer is that we learn to look to Him FIRST.

David Sought The Mind Of God On The Matter

"Then David said to Abiathar the priest, Ahimelech's son, "Please bring the ephod here to me." And Abiathar brought the ephod to David. [8] So David inquired of the Lord, saying, "Shall I pursue this troop? Shall I overtake them?" (Vs 7-8).

Pastor Richard Ham is a treasured friend. He retired after 55 years in pastoral ministry. Richard routinely concludes public prayers in an unusual way, "And give us the mind of the Holy

Ghost on all the issues of life."

I like Richard's thought process.

It only makes sense to me to pursue the woman you love. But, David took time to ask God what he should do and was rewarded with a promise.

> *"Pursue for you shall overtake them*
> *and without fail recover all."*

Do Not Denigrate Those Of Limited Endurance

> *"So David went, he and the six hundred men who were with*
> *him, and came to the Brook Besor, where those stayed who*
> *were left behind. [10] But David pursued, he and four hundred*
> *men; for two hundred stayed behind, who were so weary*
> *that they could not cross the Brook Besor,"* **(Vss 9-10).**

We are all called to equal effort. We may not be able to manage equal performance. The tithe is an easy issue from which to demonstrate this point. We may not give the same amount, but we are required to demonstrate the same level of commitment.

Assess The Value Of Unanticipated Sources Of Information

> *"Then they found an Egyptian in the field, and brought*
> *him to David; and they gave him bread and he ate, and*
> *they let him drink water. 12 And they gave him a piece*
> *of a cake of figs and two clusters of raisins. So when*
> *he had eaten, his strength came back to him; for he*
> *had eaten no bread nor drunk water for three days and*
> *three nights. 13 Then David said to him, "To whom do*
> *you belong, and where are you from?" And he said, "I am a*
> *young man from Egypt, servant of an Amalekite; and*

*my master left me behind, because three days ago I fell
sick. 14 We made an invasion of the southern area of the
Cherethites, in the territory which belongs to Judah, and
of the southern area of Caleb; and we burned Ziklag with
fire." 15 And David said to him, "Can you take me down to
this troop?" So he said, "Swear to me by God that you will
neither kill me nor deliver me into the hands of my master,
and I will take you down to this troop."   (Vss 11-15).*

Don't allow everyone opportunity to speak into your life.
Why? Not everyone you know is qualified to speak into your
life. Not every pastor, minister, or leader is qualified to speak
into your life.

Your Enemy Never Really Expects You To Attack

*"And when he had brought him down, there they were,
spread out over all the land, eating and drinking and
dancing, because of all the great spoil which they had taken
from the land of the Philistines and from the land of Judah"
(Vs 16).*

Hell wants to live in constant party mode. We are dealing with
determined, but not overwhelmingly bright adversaries. How
bright can those who chose Lucifer over Jesus really be?

Like David, We Must Expect To Get
Back Everything We Have Lost

*"Then David attacked them from twilight until the evening
of the next day. Not a man of them escaped, except four
hundred young men who rode on camels and fled. 18 So
David recovered all that the Amalekites had carried away,
and David rescued his two wives. 19 And nothing of theirs*

was lacking, either small or great, sons or daughters, spoil or anything which they had taken from them; David recovered all. 20 Then David took all the flocks and herds they had driven before those other livestock, and said, "This is David's spoil," (vss 17-20).

Activity is the proof of expectation. David went after the people under his care who had been taken captive.

Stand Against The Emergence Of Evil Among The Body Of Christ

"Now David came to the two hundred men who had been so weary that they could not follow David, whom they also had made to stay at the Brook Besor. So they went out to meet David and to meet the people who were with him. And when David came near the people, he greeted them. 22 Then all the wicked and worthless men[a] of those who went with David answered and said, "Because they did not go with us, we will not give them any of the spoil that we have recovered, except for every man's wife and children, that they may lead them away and depart," (Vss 21-22).

We must be on guard against the spirit of superiority. Men under David's command thought themselves worthy of greater reward due to their superior physical stamina. Yes, God rewards the front-line troops. But, He also rewards the people who stay at the base and provide security.

There Is Always Enough In The Kingdom

"But David said, "My brethren, you shall not do so with what the Lord has given us, who has preserved us and delivered into our hand the troop that came against

us. 24 For who will heed you in this matter? But as his part is who goes down to the battle, so shall his part be who stays by the supplies; they shall share alike." 25 So it was, from that day forward; he made it a statute and an ordinance for Israel to this day," (Vss 23-25).

The Kingdom of God is not a zero-sum equation. Our blessing does not cause others to be diminished.

25
Memories Of Mom

(Today's Teaching is Taken From Psalm 128:1; 5-6)

Anniversaries can come with some difficult emotions. But, they are connected to people worthy of celebration. Mother's Day, without having my Mom around to celebrate, is tough.

My Mom was a devout believer and someone from whom we can learn a few things about the Christian walk.

Some Facts About My Mom
1) Mom Feared The Lord.

"Blessed is everyone who fears the LORD," (Psalm 128:1).

I remember going to a party with Mom. Mother was tall, beautiful and had a great personality. She was a "Jesus girl" to the core. Her friends knew that.

I remember everyone there drinking alcohol...*except my Mom.*

"Mom," I said, "These folks don't go to church with you. Have a drink."

Her reply was one of beauty. "That may be OK for them. It is not OK for me.»

"When Jesus saved me I promised Him I would control myself. I can't do that when I drink."

The promise she made to Jesus mattered more to Mom than the implied criticism of her son.

2) Mom Walked In His Ways

"Who walks in His ways," (Psalm 128:1b).

Like many who will read this, only late in life did I appreciate the greatness of God within my Mom. Mom did not attempt to adhere to some code, although she was plagued by legalism, too.

Mom lived every day with the goal of doing her best to honor the Lord. She saw herself as literally having been saved out of hell. Few people seem to have that consciousness today. It made an incredible difference for Mom. It will do the same for us.

3) Mom Lived In The Blessings Of Righteousness

"The LORD bless you out of Zion, And may you see the good of Jerusalem All the days of your life," (Psalm 128:5).

Dad required intensive care after Mom died. Each of my five siblings joined me in visiting him daily. My first visit to Mom and Dad's house was quite moving.

The hospital bed was stored away. She will *never* need it again. But, Dad had left Mom's Bible in sight. It was still sitting open on her coffee table with a copy of my teaching notes alongside.

My Mom, "Sister Norma" as the country folks knew her, was constantly searching out the things of God. A portion of each day was spent studying the Word of God. Her later years were better than her early years because she dedicated her life to filling herself with the Word of God.

One of the best things about pastoral ministry was hearing Mom testify to her growth under my teaching.

4) Mom Enjoyed Her Children, Grandchildren and Great-Grandchildren

6 Yes, may you see your children's children. Peace be upon Israel!" (Psalm 128:6).

All my relationship with my Mom was not pleasant. Something I did not understand was a source of trouble. I felt like everyone "dumped" their kids on my Mom....*totally untrue.*

Mom loved and enjoyed her grandchildren and wanted them around her.

It was watching her interaction with her grandchildren that I came to understand something vital. We are all anointed by The Holy Spirit to do specific things. You can only truly love what you are genuinely anointed to do.

I am thankful that God Almighty, in His incredible foreknowledge, chose to make Norma Jean Blum Burton Sample my Mom.

Don't wait for a holiday to make time for your family. Do that today.

Whatever you do this day, be sure to enjoy your family.

Celebrate each other and create memories.

26
Our God of Power, Provision and Protection

(Today's Devotion is Based Upon 1 Corinthians 10:1-6)

God brought Israel out of slavery.

He ended 400 years of unimaginable bondage.

Israel left Egypt with great prosperity and total health. Not a single person was in poverty and all were in full health.

God sustained the nation by amazing examples of Divine providence. Still, Israel continually rebelled against the Lord God Almighty.

Moreover, brethren, I do not want you to be unaware that all our fathers were under the cloud, these were highly favored people.

God's literal presence was a tangible thing.

Our Lord literally kept a cloud above to protect them from the desert heat.

Years ago, I was in the Negev of Israel. The temperature was over 100F in the day. I could not believe the change during the night as the temperature dropped to the low 40's.

At night the cloud covering Israel shifted function and blazed with protective heat that moderated temperature drops and served as their national "night light."

"...all passed through the sea," (1 Corinthians 10:1a)

There have been times I have felt hemmed in. God has always brought me out in manifest victory. When Israel was trapped, God literally made a way through the ocean.

"All were baptized into Moses in the cloud and in the sea," (Vs 2)

Israel was baptized into the knowledge of Moses. The nation was also immersed in the cloud and sea. These elements foreshadow the believers' baptism that was to come.

"All ate the same spiritual food, 4 and all drank the same spiritual drink. For they drank of that spiritual Rock that followed them, and that Rock was Christ," (Vs 3-4).

Israel was provided manna. What an amazing food source! Manna, apparently, tasted as the eater wished. Manna was also a typology of the communion bread of today.

Israel had a foretaste of the streams flowing from the Rock of Ages. This stream was a spiritual type of the communion wine used in this age.

"But with most of them God was not well pleased, for their bodies were scattered in the wilderness," (Vs 5)

All Israel had to do was obey. All we have to do today is obey Obedience always produces success. Failure to do so invites certain devastation.

"Now these things became our examples, to the intent that we should not lust after evil things as they also lusted," (Vs 6)

Evil desire births evil things. There is clearly a lesson to be learned. Please join me in focusing on the things of life eternal.

27
10 Keys To Living In Victory
(1 Corinthians 1:1-10; Numbers 23:19)

"Have you got the victory today?"

It was the standard greeting in my rural home church. It is a thought that still runs through my mind and is a question I ask myself.

The Apostle Paul openly and ardently encouraged us, his readers, to make sure we are living in faith rather than blithely going along.

The question posed above should provoke thought.

My prayer is that it will cause us to grasp this important truth: *Being a Christian is sharply different from living life as a victorious believer.*

Having a home in heaven differs from living in victory on earth.

Please ponder these keys to living in victory:

1) Knowing The Will Of God For Your Life

"I, Paul, called to be an apostle of Jesus Christ through the will of God, and Sosthenes our brother,"
(1 Corinthians 1:1).

Paul was a Christian first, last and always. But, Paul was also very conscious of his leadership role in the church. Yes, he was a man who moved in revelation; a large part of that revelation was the understanding of his role as an Apostle. Paul was sent by the Holy Spirit to serve as The Apostle of The Gentiles.

Paul conducted missionary campaigns, established churches and developed leadership teams to guide each group. Clearly, Paul understood the will of God for his life.

2) Living In Sanctification

"To the church of God which is at Corinth, to those who are sanctified in Christ Jesus, called to be saints, with all who in every place call on the name of Jesus Christ our Lord, both theirs and ours:" (Vs 2).

Sanctification, in this context, refers to someone who has been set aside for God's special use and purpose. Each believer, in another element of this gift of grace, is not to just seek God's sanctification for purification from the things of the flesh.

Each Christian is to seek to discover his/her individual area of service in the Kingdom of God and become sanctified in singular focus upon this calling.

3) Walking In Grace

"Grace to you and peace from God our Father and the Lord Jesus Christ," (Vs 3).

In the universal sense, grace is the unmerited favor of God. In this specific sense, grace is the Divine enabling to live a life of peace and productivity.

4) Living In Thanksgiving

"I thank my God always concerning you for the grace of God which was given to you by Christ Jesus," (vs 4).

We can never take our salvation for granted. I am certain I am going to heaven and that will not change. However, this can never be allowed to become a state of grace-filled living for which I am unthankful.

5) Receiving His Anointing To Testify For Him

"...that you were enriched in everything by Him in all utterance and all knowledge," (Vs 5).

Yes, there are utterance gifts of the Holy Spirit. But I also believe this is a promise of a more generic manner. In addition to the manifestation gifts of the Holy Spirit, God gives each individual believer the utterance necessary to testify.

Not only do you receive overcoming power each time you testify, others are drawn to God by your words.

6) Expect The Testimony Of God To Be Confirmed In Your Life

"...even as the testimony of Christ was confirmed in you," (Vs 6)

Yes, I am to "say" I have been changed. The initial change takes place inside the convert. But, above all, the believer must live a life that reveals change.

We are not just to testify to our changed heart. We are to demonstrate the fruits of righteousness that prove a changed life.

7) Receive The Gifts God Has For You

"so that you come short in no gift, eagerly waiting for the revelation of our Lord Jesus Christ," (Vs 8).

The primary action of the Holy Spirit is revealing Jesus.

Each spiritual gift has a common element...*revealing Jesus.* How is this? The gifts reveal something Jesus has provided for believers.

8) Live A Blameless Lifestyle

"...who will also confirm you to the end, that you may be blameless in the day of our Lord Jesus Christ," (Vs 8)

All believers will stand before God in judgment. We will not be standing before Him for the determination of our salvation. We will, however, be standing before our God for the deciding of rewards.

Do not kid yourself. On that great day this truth will be important to you.

9) Depend Upon The Faithfulness Of God

"God is faithful," (Vs 9)

Our God can be depended upon. He can be trusted above all people. Consider one of my favorite Bible verses:

"God is not a man that He should lie, nor a son of man that He should repent. Has He said and will He not do? Or has He spoken, and will He not make it good?" (Numbers 23:19)

10 Enjoy Fellowship With Him

"by whom you were called into the fellowship of His Son, Jesus Christ our Lord," (Vs 9a)..

God does not just love you. God also likes you...*and wants to spend time with you.* Constantly increasing in my knowledge of Him is one of the best things about my life. My daily focus is to grow in relationship with and knowledge of Him. Reach out to know Him in a fresh way today. You will not regret your effort.

28
Require Your Emotions To Be Positive
(Today's Teaching is Based Upon 2 Corinthians 2:1-2; 12-14)

Circumstances produce.

Circumstances produce happiness. Circumstances can produce sadness. Circumstances can just produce more circumstances.

> *"But I determined this within myself, that I would not come again to you in sorrow. 2 For if I make you sorrowful, then who is he who makes me glad but the one who is made sorrowful by me?" (2 Corinthians 2:1-2).*

My daughter came home. She was gone for 19 days. She was downstairs with her mom while I was writing. They were watching "Mrs. Doubtfire." I believe that evening caused the two of them to go past 500 viewings.

What remained of a post-flight trip to *What-A-Burger* were "going away."

I still remember my emotions speaking. Thoughts of gratitude and contentment filled my mind.

Not Everyone Is In Such A Good Spot

The Holy Spirit keeps dealing with my heart. Human beings are finite and have finite emotions. But, I am so thankful the Lord of our emotions is infinite. I refuse to allow my challenges to become a burden for others.

Jesus is able to do abundantly above and beyond all we can ask or think.

Paul understood that his "yo-yoing" emotions could produce strain in the emotions of others. Paul was pleading with people to do the right thing and not require him to exert church discipline over them. Paul was saying, "I do not want to make you sad one visit and cause you to rejoice on the next. But, this is your choice."

"Furthermore, when I came to Troas
to preach Christ's gospel, and a door was opened to me by
the Lord, 13 I had no rest in my spirit, because I did not find
Titus my brother; but taking my leave of them, I departed
for Macedonia." (2 Corinthians 2:12-13)

Paul faced another choice. God had brought about "an open door." But, Paul did not find Titus behind the door. Paul had a choice to make: *Be immobilized or continue the mission?*

"Now thanks be to God who always leads us in triumph
in Christ, and through us diffuses the fragrance of His
knowledge in every place," 2 Corinthians 2:14).

I did a Daily Devotional for over 2500 days. It was emailed out to a list of a few thousand readers. During that time I received a beautiful note from a friend. This individual had never missed reading a "Daily Devotional."

This esteemed person clearly understands much of my thought process. Written words reveal thinking. By reading my words this person gets to look inside me.

On the topic of thought process, I believe, like Paul, that we Christians are destined to win. But our role involves deliberately spreading the sweet fragrance of Jesus throughout the earth.

Instead of being *ruled by* my emotions, I am *ruling over* my emotions today.

How about you? Making the choice to live on top?

The view from above is a better one.

29
Living Today...Looking Beyond
(Psalm 73:25-26;Romans 1:16-17)

A realm exists beyond the grave. The Bible openly teaches this truth.

Thoughts of heaven are plentiful for me this day. The believer has a unique series of blessings available. They are obtained by faith and require the choice to look "beyond."

It is this ability to look into the realm beyond earth that encourages us to live here.

> *"Whom have I in heaven but You? And there is none upon earth that I desire besides You," (Psalm 73:25).*

I have family and friends in heaven. But none of them have the ability to help me. Who lives in the spirit realm who can help me?

We have access to all things through The One Who orders our help, Jesus.

> *"My flesh and my heart fail; But God is the strength of my heart and my portion forever," (Psalm 73:26)*

Apart from the rapture, our flesh will fail. I do not like the idea of bodies decaying, but they do so.

The God who enables us to live on earth will receive us into heaven.

"For I am not ashamed of the gospel of Christ, for it is the power of God to salvation for everyone who believes, for the Jew first and also for the Greek," .(Romans 1:16).

I am a proud Christian. No, not "a person of faith." I am a ransomed child of God. An inestimably high price was paid for my freedom. The price of eternal freedom has been paid for all mankind.

The question remains the same, "What will we do with so great a gift?"

17 For in it the righteousness of God is revealed from faith to faith; as it is written, "The just shall live by faith."

In those fragile moments right after our Mom went to heaven, my siblings and I asked each other, "Where do we go from here?" Once the emotion subsided a bit, the pathway was clear. Mom had walked it before us. We knew we must walk the pathway of faith.

Like Mom, we have been justified by our faith in Jesus. The righteousness of God has been and will be revealed to us through faith.

This justification propels us beyond the pain of yesterday into the successes The Holy Spirit has scheduled for us today.

God has big plans for your life, dear friend...*but these plans must be sought out by faith.*

My choice is to expect and see remarkable things in God...*this day!*

30
Too Many Mentions To Ignore
(Today's Teaching Is Based Upon John 8:31-36)

Bread.

No, not the food. The band from my youth. The words are still fresh in my mind.

"If a picture paints a thousand words,

Then why can't I paint you? The words

Will never show the you I've come to know."

The beautifully descriptive song is called, "If."

"If" Is An Amazing Qualifier

1522 times.

The word "if" appears in Scripture 1522 times.

The vast majority of times "if" connects a requirement with a promise.

> *"Then Jesus said to those Jews who believed Him, "If you abide in My word, you are My disciples indeed," (John 8:31).*

Proof of our relationship with Him is conditional. Living in obedience to the Word of God proves we are His disciples. You are demonstrating one of these proofs of relationship today as you study His Word.

As we learn His Word we find ourselves moving into other areas of obedience.

> *32 And you shall know the truth, and the truth shall make you free."*

The Word of God is truth. Pontius Pilate asked Jesus, "What is truth?" Pilate was looking into the eyes of truth... *Jesus The Word of God come to earth in the flesh.*

We must be like Jesus. When Jesus came to earth He lived as a human---*depending upon The Word and The Holy Spirit.*

> *33 They answered Him, "We are Abraham's descendants, and have never been in bondage to anyone. How can You say, 'You will be made free'?"*

This verse illustrates the difference between religion and relationship. Religion is a set of rules and regulations about God.

Relationship is living in covenant with Him.

> *34 Jesus answered them, "Most assuredly, I say to you, whoever commits sin is a slave of sin.*

Sin carries with it a price. The price for salvation was paid by Jesus. The believer who continues in sin learns sin still pays a price. Jesus will not have to pay the price for sin again...*once was eternally enough.*

When we turn our backs on our Lord we find ourselves placed in a situation where we pay a personal penalty for sin through suffering.

> *35 And a slave does not abide in the house forever, but a son abides forever.*

A household slave lived inside...*so long as he was productive.*

The believer---*a love slave to Jesus*---can live in the House of God forever.

> [36] *Therefore if the Son makes you free, you shall be free indeed.*

We belong to God through spiritual adoption. Roman law allowed the oldest son to adopt brothers. Greek law stated that all slaves born in the House became family members.

Jesus adopted us. We, spiritual slaves, were born again in The House of God.

I will say and write this phrase throughout my lifetime: "*You are as free as you choose to be!*"

31
They Believed The Story
(Isaiah 11:1-2)

You probably know parts of my story. I grew up in a rural Southeast Texas community. Plum Grove is still off the beaten path, but not quite as "sleepy" now as then.

Our Texas summers can be a brutal combination of overwhelming heat and inescapable humidity. The East Fork of The San Jacinto River runs through the center of the Plum Grove community. It's waters were a welcome respite for me during my childhood years.

Frolicking in the flow was more about cooling off than exercise.

My favorite "swimming hole" was South of my Aunt Bertie's home, a place called "The Pipeline." You can guess what ran near it and how the location came by its name.

But, the community favorite was the more accessible "Buffalo Hole."

No, it was not called such because bison herds gathered there to drink.

Instead, it was home to a sizable community of Buffalo Fish. But, I digress.

Entertainment was in short supply in Plum Grove and we routinely included visits to The Sallas Grocery Store to catch up on community news/gossip.

I remember one June morning spent standing directly before an overburdened window a/c unit drinking from a bottle of Hire›s Root Beer while generally just trying to cool off.

A flustered lady whom I had never seen before strode forcefully into the store shouting loudly, "You boys will have to stop swimming in the river. A man from the State of Texas says there are seven kinds of deadly diseases active in those waters."

That ended the Summer fun for all but two of the local youth: My cousin Elmer Young, who later died tragically early in a hunting related gunshot accident, and "The Malc Man," better known today as Pastor Malcolm Burton.

Instead of going home, "Al" and I just transferred our swimming activities back to our favorite spot, "The Pipeline."

Before the day was out we were back dropping into the waters from the rope swing we had affixed to a huge Sweetgum tree that hung out over the stream. It was the same supposedly disease ravaged river. The difference: *We did not believe the report!*

I am thankful I have believed the report of The Lord. I am thankful that Isaiah believed and prophesied of Jesus.

Three Fulfilled Prophecies of Isaiah Concerning Jesus

1) Jesus Was Born Into The Human Lineage of King David

"There shall come forth a Rod from the stem of Jesse,"
(Isaiah 11:1a)

Great ladies such as Rahab and Ruth were in the human ancestry of Jesus. King David and his son Solomon were royal predecessors of our Lord.

2) Jesus Offered To Graft Us Into The Olive Tree Symbolic of Salvation

"And a Branch shall grow out of his roots," (1b)..

This experience was once reserved for Israel alone. The symbolism of this truth still speaks to my spirit today. Israel was prophetically illustrated by the domesticated olive tree. We Gentiles were represented by the wild.

I am thankful that the opportunity is now available for all mankind to be grafted into The Truth.

You and I, Gentiles, have been grafted into the Tree of Life, by faith in Jesus as Lord, Savior and King.

3) The Holy Spirit Rested Upon Jesus

"The Spirit of the LORD shall rest upon Him," (Vs 2).

It was through these manifestations of the Holy Spirit that wisdom, understanding, insightful counsel and supernatural miracles were worked. Jesus has provided everything we need to bring us into eternal life.

Jesus has also already provided everything necessary for our success in life here upon planet earth.

No, I did not believe the report of poisoned waters and I was not harmed. I am beyond thankful that I have believed and still believe *this* report.

This report contains the message of victorious living.

Share it faithfully today!